Toly A.K. 2013

Is It War?

Spring 2013, I was
visited by the spirit of
Ganesh this morning
around 5am. Thought s of
the last couple of
months thick and heavy
on my brain, with the
place that had to make
out a living went ablaze
after 20 years, Vinny.
Being let out of the
pen, and thoughts of
Paris.

They say hindsight is
20/20. This remains to
be true, hopefully not
just for me but for the
naysayers and critics. A
brave girl told me once
to do something for me,
so here ya have it.

The male whores world

line up at the burger
shack in San Francisco's
East side. I can't
escape the feeling that
that's where every good
gigolo goes to die, and
I'd be forced into
making a porn one day
soon.

In my vision, Ganesh was
crouched in prayer, his
tusks white and boney
and skin deep grey. I
take it to mean a future
which is unknown to me.
To turn the on the past.

Odds against me, roll
the dice, even though
I'm not a gambler.

I found a pair of fifty
dollar sneakers; little
did I know they were
cleats. The good thing
is no one will be able
to give a fake imprint
of my shoe in a murder.
A guy tried to show me
his gun. I didn't put my

finger prints it, it
stank of set up. He
could commit a crime
with my prints on the
gun and I'd do his time.
I don't think so, sorry
bud. Hang a fix; frame a
picture, not a guy.

Break a leg they said,
then a Taurus ran me
over, fucking up my
right leg. It's not bad
enough they had given up
on life by buying a Ford
Taurus but they had to
run over an artist on
top of it.

In retrospect maybe I
should take back the
cleats, but it's funny,
I can give a guy a swift
kick in the rear and
he'll remember it. Or
kick a serious asshole
in the face for ganging
up on me.

The kink in my back has
gotten worse since the

accident; it makes me
feel quite frail, may do
an adularian psychosis.

It's a ubiquitous game
of who's tougher, more
man, tuff on tuff. Ken
and Barbie go all around
the world, plugged in
every hole.

What clothes you gonna
wear?

When you fake your
death?
Your own funeral?
That's $2500 a casket,
that's what you're
worth, the wood you're
going to rot in as the
maggots knarl inside
you. You Frankenfurter,
you. Chop up scrutinize,
diseased impudent worm.

The French believe Jesus
once resurrected, moved
to France, and sired
children.

I'm Ophiuchus, the one
of the hurricane. Born
of Memphis, with as
guide.

There's the highway. The
meeting of Ophiuchus
takes place with the
moon in half silver on
the new dawn.

Such a necromantic, I
had a crazy ass porn
dream with three
corpses. They were
sucking on my fingers in
their mummy delight, a
fricassee of undead.

Licensed to the Goya
painting of Saturn
eating his son, the
fashionably on time
where everyone's late an
hour.

Once again the industry,
the machine tried taking
me out, but I just got a
j.o.b. On the side.

Possibly waiting for me
to get shot by a cop, or
bottoming out in porn.
Like girls in porn like
fucking anyway.

They're gay anyway, so
are strippers. They
sleep with men for
money. You know diamonds
are girls' best friend
apparently, said the
blind man to his deaf
wife.

What's new a mild case
of autosclorosis making
you a medium for a day?

My hoarder, whore
mongering family still
talks to the television
and want me to get the
drip from a whore to
become a "man".

Set aside the
Preparation H sharing,
an old jar of peanut
butter became the day's
topic, and the

depression, rotten
fruit? An old saw oiled
to the nines still with
no parts in the shop
will apparently work to
chop down our oxygen
support system while
caregiver the clubbed
seal pelt of our lives.

From a neo-nazi cult who
hates WWII veterans, a
Jewish person gave me
some K-ching-double-no-
no! Unearth the Robert
Plant DVD and hear the
war cry of geek Greek
old men hyperventilating
that he's too sexy for
songs.

Another method of
reprogramming Christian?

The Vedic also follows
the signs of Ophiuchus
and accepts them whole
heartedly unlike black
albinos whose limbs are
game pieces on the chess
board in parts of Africa

or the mulatto mix of
ethnics who make good
porn stars after you ass
rape them!

The Vizier, the Oracle
sometimes depicted as an
"it", he-she, with an
overbearing mother
figure in Fellini movies
will do a dance on your
grave.

Is it war, between the
spiritual and the human?

Made in a cheap hotel
for four hour
honeymooners on the
south side of Montreal
with a heart-shaped bed
and cheap wine to feed
and keep the
Bacchanalian spirit
happy, to appease the
Gods of Saturnus!

The fear is of writers,
they'll end up like
Aesop.

Sworn into slavery and
drudgery in the now but
writings continue.

My vindication vending
pieces of my fingers in
the food to give the
cannibals a good taste
and the shakes.

My folks are still
trying to get rid of the
calluses on my hands and
feet from manual labour,
the forced concentration
camps of today.

Pure liberalism is
social equality, but we
live in a capitalist
haven of cutthroats and
brigands-corsair!

Fair Ophelia, show us
your bosom, the masses
cry, spread in the name
of oblivion, lead us
into temptation for my
name was the words
spoken by and to the
serpent- meanwhile a

girl in a black
turtleneck is the rage;
"Tomorrow's a drag, man,
a king size bust."

Role playing "Night of
the Hunter" the dead
aqua lung body at the
bottom of the lake.

"Good"- "Evil"
Parameters of folklore
for an uncivilized world
based
on Gaia and Nun,
Sumerian lore to the
cattle, keep them herded
and yield good crop.

Man's inherent need to
cannibalize and destroy
each other; will it
reach to the stars and
planetary
constellations?

There is "no war" in
space just capitalism.

The bourgeoisie plan to
defeat, to build condos

on the space station so
that they can drink a
cafe au lait and have a
Danish on Mars and make
it with an alien hooker,
a lactating Venus-
"Electric".

A Boticelli in a garbage
pit, sewer, pissing
vanilla for mechanic
masturbating to a
melancholy romance made
to unearth the undead of
Aesclepius and Herod,
paying strict attention
to foot note the
philosophy of Jung.

Got gas will travel,
Poofta, H Scrofa tou
diabolou.

Welcome to Purgatory!

Man's earthly delights,
Rae Dawn Chong in "Quest
for Fire".

Her-Rod, a punk chick's
dick, the great builder

who killed his family;
to cut off one's nose to
smite his face and
rebuild the ultimate sex
machine woman, at the
end of the rapture, the
lunacy of pimped out
fashion. When the norm
is to shaft for the
million dollar deal.

Another flip of the coin
for old Rosencrantz and
Guildenstern, the
helioscope projects.

I Serpenterian, the veil
lifted, the heliotrope
in mourning. " The Night
of the Iguana" the
Lolita of the Biblical
equation.

Man's obsession "the
chase is better than the
catch" when old cougars
are whacking off young
hairless boys in back
alleys, what do you make
of the world when
you're,

Jane wants a dick from a man-ho? "Mr. Christian, the bounty is my ship." "No, there is a mutiny I say."

I always wondered why you are always dating one another, I'm sure, Yea verily it weighs heavy, as soon as I knock you up, you'll get stuck in a kitchen because mankind has deemed immigrant sons unfit for office work in fear of hearing men talk about black people and immigrant sons. I can go undercover as a white guy and record dialogue in my mind with ease, like I'm a dumb Daigo wop who wants to be English but too chicken to get a tattoo, so I wear Ed Hardy.

Carolina went after the long green and ended up

in a hearse.

I gave her a ride to her
place and she shoved her
hot smoky tongue down my
throat. Last I saw of
her.

Didn't end up going to
the free mason meeting.
Cut my finger awful bad
though at work,
releasing endorphins
which tickeled me pink.

You are the Zoroaster,
said the Charlemagne to
a burning empire
"Don't be a word?" I
returned knowing full
well I was in no power
position. I rule with
pen and paper, the silk
imported from the Middle
East from rotten wood
not the backs of silk
worm.

I'm more likened to
taking a set of brass
knuckles to my

neighbour's head for
dropping the n bomb and
projecting " take a
piss" nightly, so that
he will deeply
understand the cut that
will not heal in the
physical and go " on his
ass" with a power
drill.

A dream you can't wake
up from like having acid
thrown at you in a
shopping mall, hitting
you in the face, because
a girl's giving you
crazy ass porn dreams.

Salvador Dali exposes
his brain, have cut like
a monkey brain feast
from the middle of the
earth with some weird
tropical climate that
produces huge bugs and
documentaries like
"faces of death". The
feces to rot your
teenage camping trip to
Disneyland.

Escaping the edict of
what your parents want,
society wants to make of
you and "the void" the
space after university
and finding a j.o.b.
Denying all associations
with "The Graduate" and
Mrs. Robinson, of
course.

Ritalin babies become
anti-social misers that
want to be wiser with
the collegiate flunky
attitude that displaying
your art is prostituting
your work- that is of
course until there is
and displayed filtered,
pilfered and
regurgitated in the five
senses of the .

Your haematosis
undefined, metastasizing
hemoblobus at an
anabolic rate that make
your dopamine surge
inconsistently, the

little receptors in your
pineal dying out making
your chi unbalanced?

Take a breath from
what's already there,
CO2 reconverted by the
Amazon rainforest you
clear cut to build a
golf course for
philandering six figure
politicians who pocket
tax dollars, while you
tell little kids the
power lies in the hands
of "mystic pizza" sewn
on the back of a
mushroom cloud.

The diastolic rate of
the Dionysian cult,
humping in rapture to
thrill the chronic
masturbator. The diocese
of the rich and famous
reliving Dostoyevsky's
wet dream, an epitaph
that keeps the bug house
reeling.

"Can't beat the suicide

rate," she said.

Mount Vesuvius erupts in
a wet bukaki dream.
Plato is sitting in a
mound of butter melting
in a pot with fifty
pounds of lard on his
back, stuffing a
shilling in a
leprechaun's arse, the
master manipulator
directing traffic from
the bottom of a tequila
sunrise wet with the
hot, damp, musky stench
of unabashed perversion
of power.

When it rains, it pours,
the lightening coming
down- ten twisters in
Texas say it three times
fast. Ten twits taking
turns on Tallulah Bank
head's corpse.

A Van Dyke portrait of
nothing more than your
bureaucratic
deliverance?

Affluent in verse and
structure from the
punctured vein, as I
reign in stigmata of
your Christ's pose.

The river a coin toss
away.

The red robin sis on its
perch outside my door on
a thin electrical wire,
as the lamplighter hums
an ode, a melancholy
dirge in your vibrator's
tentacle the arpeggio
wet to massage the clit
of Vanessa del Rio on a
sex rampage with a truck
driver at the Am/Pm.

The- heir to Cleopatra's
throne disrobes in the
city park from
underneath a tanned,
stained trench coat to a
gang bang girl's rhyme-
void of alliteration and
the Pentecostal church's
pretext of fine moral

judgement.

To the Toltec's words
can be your art form,
but one might say
"you're dead on the
word." A ptolemic
solution.

"Old bog-what's it
from?" Snap! Fact or
fiction?

The thorny rose pierces
the iron man's flesh,
with a broken heart to
transcend the post
apocalyptic landscape to
fit the bill with a
narcissistic drawl
befitting his I.D. He
wanders desert plains
with a sworn of wit and
dysfunction.

Malpheasant.
Harbringer.
Dissident aggressor.

How many times can you
use "I" in a sentence?

Franciscan monks hum a
Gregorian chant, nodding
to the baptismal urn, in
parallax, modern
secularism.

The shovel sits by the
male tree, sharpened and
ready to skewer the head
off the Leviathan, a
cabalist grave.

"Be an optimist,
alchemist, pessimist,"
she said.

"How many sides does a
quadrilateral triangle
have?" I ask.

Sepentarius, the healer.

"Knock, knock."

"Who's there?"

"Oiling the barrel," he
said

"That's not the

password," I say.

The man wet with
deception drives the
stake into stomach,
sapuko, hara kiri, the
fallen ronin – hangs
from his intestines the
mandrake picked from the
virginal hand of
innocence.

The flower of Immaculate
Conception on the lire's
machine head, a liar's
spelling of yore?

The pine needle pierces
the honeycomb, the
antithesis of pectin in
syrupy mass of molasses
into the pill shovels
gullet.

Smell-O-Rama, porn
theatre, worshipping
glory holes in the basin
of the south, as
tweaking fuck-nuts pray
for Mary's assumption,
consuming to the gills

of forlorn antiquity.

Four score and seven
years ago, you learned
the word, and like the
hell that you are,
produce drug induced
comas, to circumnavigate
the radius of a square.

Can you fit a square pig
in a round hole?

Anachronism?

Eclectic, diversion from
the mundane, robot,
routine existence of the
trenches of dreary
existence.

"Learn to spit more
vehemently," he said to
his deaf wife.

Cliché rhetoric of
metaphor of neo-
classical stereotype of
the tragic hero
exemplified by the eye,
stolen from the during a

drunken bar brawl over a
rib steak dinner and a
plush pitre?

The horny swallow burps
out the worm, "chirp,
chirp".

Put a guy in a suit, he
forgets high school
history. You're the
immigrant who came off
the from for crimes
unknown to form a socio-
society condemning
everyone with a fuckin
j.o.b.
Fighting corruption from
the end of a crack or
meth pipe in pure
vigilante form, from the
arse-end badge of your
rent-o-cop uniform.

When internalized costs
exceed those of the free
market you're left your
r.v., home, s.u.v., and
fluent teeth marks
instead of your morning
blowjob.

The collective
unconscious of Jung. The
aftermath still dormant
in the archetype of "buy
now!" world.

Melanomer, Melanoma for
the melancholy, sitting
in Bukowski fashion
reaching for a now life.

"It's a struggle," she
said, "If you pry your
face apart and drink
deep you can see your
skull." Don't forget to
your porsche. Your
demeanour? Liken to a
semi hitting you up.
With a need for wolves
bane, little red riding
hood?

Sylvia Plath shoves her
head in the oven to keep
from rolling over in her
grave.

So I ask, "Is it war?"
between the spiritual

man and the norm. I
figure the worlds at
war, by divine right I
have earned my place,
will the bourgeois
accept Ophiuchus? Or
will they drive them and
me out!

I'm not a war-like
person; after all I wear
plaid not an army coat.
War pigs still have the
power, the masses no
longer walking through
life with blinders on.

The pitchfork hits the
hard earth, a new yield
for the harvest; Gaia
and Nun are appeased
with the sacrifice.

To go beyond the
parameters emotion and
the every day life- to
transcend, to pass
beyond the limits of
understanding, and
despotism was founded on
free principles but God-

fearing people still
believe in a good
beating and everyone
with a tattoo is a whore
or a conman.

The cobweb-like Gordian
knot- the final wave
will come to you like a
tsunami of subsistence.
The orgiastic delight in
Caligula-like fashion,
Rasputin meets
Constantine, and crowns
you higher to God than
Vizier by right of womb.
The lion paw close to
heart, the formations of
sight and sound in one's
mind.

Is the universe real,
Cartesian question,
"something from
nothing," I said.

He stared blankly,
enraged.

"Why does there have to
be something if there's

nothing?" I say.

The physical parameters
are they real or are we
living in a dream, in a
kind of embryonic womb
waiting to awake?

"Stay objective," one
says.

"Is that possible?" I
retort.

If the universe isn't
real then are we
constructs of a higher
being,
of God each person an Id
in a God's mind?

The idea of God was
passed down from
primitive societies
worshipping the sun and
the harvest, maybe it
just is.

"What is?" One says.

"Just that," I say.

A leaf falls on one of
my paintings of Ganesh
as I'm painting a leaf.

FIN

29

"Death Republica-when
the sun meets the earth"
Toly a.k. 2013

Won't catch me
smiling about something
gross, like anchovies.

The brain probe
ship flew past my
window, as I looked into
the rusty mirror and saw
my myself as a half dead
zombie-the babes lay
asleep in their wombs ,
half tucked and all in a
row. The projection on
the wall illuminating
their inner durra into
nocturnal dreamy land.

If Romeo and Juliet
was a symbiotic creature
would they be more
Capulet?

The fin on the
sphere of the Sisyphus
medicine ball rolls

around the shack,
resting on the spider
brains – the crackers
den.

Half between a mass
of a great orgy in the
sky while juggling
vaginas on my nine cocks
as finger sucking undead
corpse women coat my
slumber.

Another fine day,
discovering my allergy
to sunlight has filtered
through with it yet.
Thinking I worked out
that bug, I've proceeded
to walk a country mile-
daily-the antithesis of
which was dreaming I was
I was a crawly thing
creeping into an
elevator with a rich
lady, to escape the
confines of a large
prison garage where I
was chopped up,
grounded, through an
assembly line.

Maid Marianne, I
think we're being duped
and its time for some
fancy footwork through
Sherwood forest.

Time to grow a
moustache and perm my
hair and go super fly.

The transistor
radio buzzing in my ear,
barreling out gossip.
Wavelengths travel
through space, do they
travel through rock. Are
we doing damage to the
planet by thinking, is
thought matter to be
pierced and diced?

A giant steel rod
cuts through the earth's
core to tap into the
precious magma, another
bright idea.

Pain dolls on an
excursion from the
elusions fields, kind of

like, pickin the flower
pedals "she loves me,
she loves me not", know
what I'm sayin'
"je t'adore, jet a –
adore."

    With a jawbone and
a spear. Meanwhile back
home at the ranch,
American criminals are
planning crimes in
Canada to bring down the
Canadian dollar with a
cyclopean albino kitty.

The tempest turns on an
ensanguined smile from
the ludicrous drool the
spills from the gullet
of herpes lined -lipped
kiss of the ten buck pop
in the back of the
hearse, hey dipshits is
your noodle wet on the
internet trick being
dpd'd in silver nitrate,
the cavern hides many
ghosts macabre, an
anthem, anathema bred to
feed the underworld as

the offed breed slave
modem dilemmas piss from
the disgruntled mail
clerk in the wall mart
uniform that breeds the
psychotic slur under the
thumb of the badly
coiffed head still under
the beatnik beat, the
breed still torrent with
the bullet that pangs
for the easy life-
disillusioned with the
impudence of the burn
out seer that never
crossed the whirl of,
this shell too much for
my rotting corpse
injected with sleep long
gone psychotic on the
page, buzzed out
thinking of the kink of
the elbow pounding skull
into swelled mass of
blood clotted-fucked up-
what the fuck, the
filtered dissection that
warped the pineal,
begging for the
exhibitionist to warm
the retina and

stimulate.

July, 2013-what can
I say, during the lunar
eclipse or some shit the
place next to where we
meeked out a living in
my youth went up like
splinters; it's already
up again though.
Bored out of my skull
otherwise. N.E.W.S. is
coming to Montréal.
Probably bringing a
storm with him.

Highway is calling.

Poem for Sarah:
Standing out in the
cold.
It biting at our being.
Rubbed noses under a hot
flash of gas.
I felt my body go warm.
With a shudder from
deaths kiss.

Tried to sell a
camera on a social

internet site and was
inundated with chrome
crank wings, hell bent
on reversing the coin.

Uncles got a tumor,
may be cancer, i'm still
chain-smoking.

With no hope for a
re-write of "white
chicks -I hate immigrant
sons." Paranoiacs
reigning supreme
thinking one or the
other is the butt of a
joke, the mindfuck that
keeps the ratings
machine rolling.
The old man still sits
in his lawn chair, still
drinking whiskey from a
coffee mug under an old
apple tree. An apple,
ripe on the vine, falls
to his feet.

"The silence"-the
bug in your ear, the
crickets. The odd
passerby is a far cry

from the junky pissing
on the floor in the
ghetto. Still no such
thing as silence. The
hiss of the projector as
an old time movie plays
out in my head. A train
and a baby black fawn in
hunters lodge. The wild
boar bites down on the
sinews of a trap as an
axe falls down on its
head.

Strange visitor in
the morning- a weird
conch, lobster-like
alien floating creature
was hovering above me
watching. The usual
greeting from the
Neanderthal, I tried to
belt it, and then it
disappeared. I took a
leak. I went outside
motioning for it to
follow as if it were in
some cloaking mode.
outside, I proceeded to
have smoke and eyed it
with one eye, whistled

the theme to close
encounters, then patted
my head and rubbed my
belly while singing
"wild child" by
w.a.s.p., I don't know
why this tune, it was
lame to me but it made
me laugh.

Alien invasion!

Dreams of a dark
castle and a secret
people in the know who
have lasted a long time
but kept separate from
the squirrelly masses. I
tune in on an imaginary
radio and hum the tune
to the old Hanna
barberra cartoon, "the
jetsons".

A Doberman barks in
a mans face, the man
transforms into a
Rotweiller. My dog barks
at the screen in the
movie house.

A young girl tries to calm him down, my dogs freakin! What I'm doing with a dog in a movie house, I'm not sure…

"Pychotropica"- we try to exit the movie house but the only exit is through a pile of toddlers in a narrow encavement.the leash slips out from my hands and my dog races ahead to the other side. Something grates my feet and yanks me back in. I find myself buying popcorn, they are serving sausages. I ask for some chocolate after some girl asks for waffles in a plastic wrap.

The cashier seems annoyed that the girl likes me, and I find myself in a factory with the ghost of her mother

killing a man who was
her murderer in a
painting of a narrow
stairway leading to a
basement warehouse.

Pipes are being
thrown from the ceiling
cut and thrown. H is
freaking', "you're out
of here, Missy!"

I'm supposed to
escort this punk girl on
a cocaine binge out of
the half way house we're
staying in. missy tells
me she loves me and
doesn't want to leave.

I sit down on the
floor and let her know
she's lying, and ask her
if she has a place to
stay.

She says yes and
exits through the window
into the snow, as if
she's breaking into the
outside world to steal
her life back.

I awake with a
start in parent's
basement with a thick
feeling in my spine.

The sink in the
bathroom has been ripped
off the wall and water
is spewing, par tout.
My feet are cold
and wet on the ceramic
floor.
The old man sits on
his lawn chair, drinking
whiskey from a coffee
mug. Under an old apple
tree. An apple, ripe on
the vine, falls to his
feet.

Crystal jumps out
of bed says something in
Spanish, I hear her
brother walking around
upstairs, so I jet.

Mary-Shelley laughs
from her couch as her
mothers footsteps are
heard upstairs. She is

naked except for a pink
robe. I dart out his
front door. The townies
have gathered out front
with their pitchforks
ready to kill
Frankenstein's little
monster, sir cum a lot.

Some mandrake is
growing at the foot of
my bed.

A fang tooth
sharpened, to bite the
flesh of the shadowy
vision.

I close the clip on
H's flower set corset as
she rubs her sore neck,
I can see her far eyed
through the mirror.
They say the mirror
is the window to the
soul, like all timeless
madness in space, I see
reflections through her
vanity.

Your time of Dorian

gray, life of Pan from
Greek myth or weird
experimental films from
Kenneth anger.

Anais Nin sweet to
the touch of the
imagination of gentle
words on page.

"Bring out the
brute!" she shouts.

I, clasped in
shackles in a cage, hang
high above the oratory.
The organist plays the
tune. A bloody tear
streaks down Jesus' eye.

The world in siege
as the bomb erupts.

Picasso is in his
tomb still painting. His
skeletal corpse lifts a
boney finger.

Corporate jargon
spews out of the NASDEX-
telling you to grow up-

think and live your life
according to multi
millionaires way of
life, who are so
disassociated with the
zealot infidels called
"common man" working
minimum wage, or not at
all-why? Why should I
work to fill your pocket
on the dirty boulevard?
Am I your butler? I want
to you're your carcass
to shreds, hand your
head on a spike in my
front yard, eat your
organs and bury your
children alive, like
Genghis khan.

The bumble bee
buzzes around the large
plant crustation that
emits a blur of pollen,
mutated into a
gargantuan "little shop
of horrors" bottomeless
belly of dysentery mouth
to feed o an obese,
bulimic ghetto belly.

"Cant get enough of that sugar crisp?"- Crunch with punch. The man pour out the honey from the honey bear jar looking deep inside the honey comb s hive mind for answers through a drugged out haze- the literal cohesion thought at Eton far beyond his grasp, in his stupor.

"Knock knock, who's there?"

They see him lurking in street corners, Hyde.
A clown rubs a balloon.

One eye trained on hell or heaven?

Cyber psychedelic sex fuck. Thoughts to prelude the epilogue-a dissertation in the buccinator-the scowl forlorn in ambiguity, with no cause.

"They're tearing me apart!" the rebel howls.

Another day another hour.

"Murderers! Murderers!" as she swallows the pill bottle.

The clock keeps ticking, a wet dream to feast on, sublimated in subdivisions.
Until the sun meets the earth, we will be as one.
The war machine churning, thoughts thick about romance.
Bus ticket one hundred bucks to go down south. Maybe meet up with E.W.slum it for abit. Can't beat this consumption; capital cough. Lorry this is a real fine mess.

Any hopes of making another linear film seemed squashed.

The modern fascination with cop lawyer doctor dramas is too deeply ingrained in pop culture, further enforcing a police state.

That's twenty one films in five years on a tour across Canada in a project call "under new management" I haven't seen a dime from

The prevailing thought is why give money to Greeks in the arts, I suppose. Twenty one films, i've made, one great hoark, a "fuck you" o the who's who's. The public relations people who churn out formula based on survey of polo clad people. No requests. No icons. No effigies.

The philanthropist spiels an empty feeling-hitting the highway. in search of…

Almost got run over by a p-up on my way down the block. World war ultra violet begins.

That's about when I met the "sugar twins". They were both once addicts but have resorted to chewing down on chocolate and drinking a lot of moo juice. I could swear one of them is a serial killer but it's hard to say which one, the male or the female. Both have admitted to sticking things in their orifices, like brushes, curling irons. Not hot. That would hurt. Peeing in the shower. I'm sure

a Mormon girl gone bad
will visit soon claiming
one of her many
husbands.

Bad? Kind of like,
flirting with the ghost
of Tallulah bankhead, in
the spirit of the fame
whore.

We sat in the café,
eating butter cakes.
Marie, twin one, let's
break his arm!" Johnny,
twin two he's too
pretty, let's punch him
in the face until he
dies!"

I turn to them,
"would you two turn that
damn video game off?"

Marie,"ever notice
how a video game is a
reflection of a life you
are leading?"

"Uh, no" I retort.
They don't respond.

Quite frankly I should probably dig a shallow grave for them both because it's the least they'd do for me.

The old man is now sitting at the dinner table. The table has a half sawed off leg stitched together with duct tape. He chokes on a fishbone and screams something at his wife.

He then walks outside with whiskey in his coffee mug, a lone apple falls from the tree in his yard, as he sits back into his chair.

Secret agent 13 adjusts her thigh high stockings under her coat. A pouty blonde huffs from behind a cigarette. She says in a smokey voice," good bye."

13 pulls her close
and the girl digs
her half bitten
paint chipped nails
into 13's face and
breaks away.
From my motel room,
I sit, with the
curtain half drawn
and adjust twin
ones holster, "dig
it."
I say. "One shot
the head, you
savy?"Twin one
says, "Stop being
the voice inside my
head!"
       "Devil locked
on to the chip on
your shoulder,
little one, you get
one shot, after
that all hell
breaks loose" I
say.

       13 enters a
blown Chevy, with

shivs for a
laxative-I guess
that car would hit
the bowel not, not
sure. The pouty
blonde see the
glare from the
laser sighting,
throws secret agent
13 a look. 13 jumps
in the back seat
and withdraws a
sawed off shot gun
from a bay crib,
shoots through the
window at twin one
high above.
"Sugar," she says.
She turns to me but
I was never there."
always the brides
maid, never the
groom! 13 huffs and
kicks the door
opens of the Chevy.
The pouty blonde
says, "Who's
that?"13 answers,
"sugar twin."

        The old oaf

turns to his wife
and screams at her,
"turn the damn TV
off!"

Hopes dashed
of being on the
road.

What will be,
will be..What were
still is with which
witch it was. Lose
my mind over a pin
up queen? Id rather
not be laughing at
the murnau moment,
or der blu Engel.

Glory, had my
hair good and
greasy, now it's
cropped all the way
down, and i'm
hiding out in a
little 8x8 room.
Lil'swamp girls
callin'. I hear her
say, "Hear me
roar."

Midnight-flick
my bic.

I turn on to a
thousand joys of
celestial nods of
the abyss and
return to the
mundane tasks of
keeping keeping the
grass green where
men and women are
laid out to pasture
for the morning
rush to work as
they fall in line,
one behind another.

The government
regurgitating us in
its five bellies
and chewing on our
entrails, slowly,
like cud.

Secret agent
13 makes out with
the pouty blonde on
t.v."I'm leaving
you, she says.I
turn off the TV.

Eaten alive by
the profits of
"cool".

I'm three
times seven and
weigh seventy four
pounds. The
dwarfword from
Quebec a backward
son of a bitch.

Snap, Martha!
The well worn
stairs. Are you
afraid?

Human-like
lamas are adding
hair and tattoos to
ancient Amazonian
sculptures as a way
to communicate with
an alien species.
Defacing ancient
ruins as a mockery
of our human old
form, and
"function"-arte we
really meant to

serve in the market
place? to exist
only for the soul
reason of making
money and buying
"stuff" or are we
,meant for a higher
purpose in the
universe?

An albino cat
crosses my path in
the wake of a full
moon, then a black
cat.

The wind
outside my window
howls words of love
but when I exit
there is no wind.

The howls
waken me at four
am.

I light a
smoke.

I notice
dishcloth,

underwear with the
ass cut out of it
and wonder, why?

It's the
bronze age" he says
with a snarl
"We're salvaging
copper for the
scrap yard" I
retort.

"Copper,
bronze-whatever."

I light a
smoke outside.

A smoke stares
at me then trots
off.

I scramble for
more smokes; a cop
drives past but
doesn't stop me.

I'm almost on
hundred per cent
sure the cathode
ray tube is causing

a rift in the space
time continuum.
It's possible that
i'm receiving
gossip from Lucille
ball in the undead
s quest to rein
habit the globe
with comedy and
chocolate.

Maybe catch a
werewolf disease
from a tattoo.

Maybe buy a
black caprice and
write versus of the
revelations on it.

Evolove.
Lovevol.
Devilived.

It was once
said, "The mirror
reflects cosmic
humor."

"Cosmic."
The cosmos.

I'd like to
shoot out into
space, into the
crowd of the
cosmos.

Dwarfed.
Forward.
Foreword.

Forelorn in
the aftermath. I
flick my bic, an
heat up a quarter
and toss it at a
rich man getting
out of a b.m.w., he
picks it up and
burns his finger
tips.

Sitting in
court with a heel
busted out of my
snappy shoes. I
feel like i'm in
court for whoring
my ass on st.
Laurent, all this
to contest a ticket

for working. I
plead insanity to
working and the
judge throws the
case out of court,
instead of calling
it a travesty to
the justice system.

The old man
pours whiskey into
the coffee mug. The
sugar twins have
taken to calling me
knucklehead or
swampy.

I run onto the
side walk
pretending to trip,
and on a woman
breast, grappling
it firmly in my
palm.

Her name is
Victoria, but
quickly calls me a
queen for trying to
get her into the
sack with that

dirty old
trick."Rubbish"I
say.

Another
sleepless night,
with a man
screaming down the
block, bashing he
brains out of a
Buick with a bat,
maybe the guy with
the car owes the
guy some money?

I'm on my way
to the office
cosmipotluck when a
car pulls overt and
a young thug gets
out and barfs on
his hands and
knees. Praying to
the bowel gods.

Three am, the
witching our. Moons
in half sliver.
Sign of the
Ophiuchus overhead,
connecting the

little dipper to
the big dipper.

In my dream
Victoria slides
down a fire escape
and into the gutter
that i'm sleeping
in.
I wake up in
my old mans
basement, not aware
of how I got there;
guess they scooped
me off the sidewalk
again.

Sitting at the
dinner table, I
take the nib out of
the pen and spit a
paper spit ball at
one of the sugar
twins; he screams
he'll kill me in an
old fashioned way,
perhaps implosion.

"I'm abreast
of the situation" I
retort.

Much like the
drawing of freud
"whats on a mans
mind?"

"You will
perish", she says.

The bush
outside my door
catches fire; it
leans to the side
and falls over. I
smolder the flames
with the heel of my
worn boot.

"Pent up
Penguin," I may be
becoming.
"Choke on a
spit ball, "he
says.

The giant head
stares back at me
with a toothy grin.
I snip the tip off
his bearded chin
and have at the god

wheel again.

Pain is a four
letter word-fuck-
kill-love.

Woke up this
morning had one
black sock on, one
white sock.

Videotron came
on the tube, a high
tech digitally 3d
rendered
transvestite. "We
are living in a
police state,
fuck."She cussed

"This is
w.w.u.v.-world war
ultraviolet-park it
up right!"

Something
about having a
white soc and a
black sock on made
me want to walk in

a straight line,
not wonky. The yin
yang of defeat, is
knowing you're
through before you
begin but going
ahead with it
anyway.

"You might be
a pretty girl, why
don't you blow on
my dice?" I add

"A creative
person would have
tattooed his
testicles-as dice I
mean to say." She
says smirking.

"Now that
would be real good
luck," I add.

I know
somewhere in a
small rural town of
Transylvania there
is a woman growing
a horn and they're

calling her Satan.

I walk into
the psychology
clinic and lie down
on the couch in
front of Dr.
Morrison. He asks,"
Tell me about your
mother."

"well, its
like threes a
string behind her
back that's
attached to her
mouth, that someone
unleashes
constantly, her
ceaseless agonizing
nagging would make
the sanest person
on earth commit
suicide or mass
genocide-commit a
crime to make money
to get away from
her. Luckily I
understand the
psychology behind
over bearing

mothers or id be
walking around in a
pretty little
frock. She told me
a story once about
biting the head off
a chicken and
watching the body
flail around the
farm, or about
drowning kittens in
a toilet bowl
slowly breaking
each one of their
necks," I say.

He says,
"That's an
interesting story,
but I can't tell
how much of it you
invented and how
much is fact."

I assure him
its all true and
its not the
painkillers
talking, the
prescription he
filled for the rib

ripped out of me to
create an alien
symbiotic creature
of Romeo an Juliet
to live out their
life seeking
revenge on their
families, like
herod.

He turns and
laughs.
"Mr. Morrison,
"i ask, "what your
first name?"
James" he
says.
"What are you
kidding?" I ask
again.
"I assure you
its all true and
not a sub plot of
hubba bubba chewing
gum vs. the alien
creature.
He chuckles.

Chapter 2

Daffy and

Taffy were our pet
ducks while growing
up. They'd keep me
fresh on ripe eggs,
that I would eat
raw.

We'd play the
quack quack game.
Id say, "quack,
quack", they'd
quack back. This
would amuse me for
hours or until
Laverne and Shirley
would come on the
tube. One night
after the
babysitter was
turned off after
massaging my
cortex, a meal of
chicken was served.

I asked why it
was rubbery and why
it was brown.

The next day,
daffy and taffy
were gone and I was

whisked off to the
barber shop to get
a mullet.

Sick and tired
of being sick and
tired.

Having a hard
time reading girls
signals, I think
one wants more but
shed rather
strangle me than
fuck, or it may be
an id from
childbirth seeing I
was born with an
umbilical chord
around my neck.

Seems like the
worlds crumbling
out from under our
feet, people still
get up, go to work,
in line, fall in
line.

Art school
taught us to look

at things with
child like eyes but
when you talk to a
kid or try to raise
one you quickly
realize our
generation is naïve
compared to threes.
They're barraged by
media,
desensitized; some
have realife
experiences though,
"damaged", like me.

    An apple sits
next to a tree,
which is now a
stump. A chainsaw
sits on the old
mans lap next to a
broken coffee mug.

    The old house
creaks as if
something's afoot.

    The game
"populous" reigns
down on the
debauchery of my

forefathers.

"Belle rive."
Must hold down the
fort, without
wayward school
girl's visiting-
with my father
doing his best
uncle jeb, Stanley
Kowalski
impersonation.

I check into a
motel next to a
strip club. Figured
id party all night
and then crash.
Little did I know
that id enter into
a coma-like sleep.

That's where I
met her.

The dream
girl, sandman she
comes, my nocturnal
mistress of the
deep to breath
whispers in my ear.

In a cloudy
blue room I can see
her sitting at a
desk, through a
round portal in my
mind as if through
a looking glass or
a mirror on the
wall.

I was driving
once and had and
had a vision of
several portals
such as these
opening up into
bedrooms, like an
old school movie
playing out in my
head.

A giant
whimsickle wand
spun around and
corralled a million
people who appeared
to me as little
iridescent beings
of energy. Then I
saw the void of

space surrounding
us all. Giant
nebulas and suns. I
try to wake from my
sleep. My neck
cracks in my pillow
but not really, I
try to shake off
the feeling

Same 8x8 room.

The old man is
walking down the
street with the
chainsaw. He comes
up to the sugar
twin's house and
saws their front
door n half. Walks
up the bedrooms and
leave two big
bright red apples
on each of their
bed stands. They
keep themselves
covered under their
blankies, hiding
from the boogeyman.

Don't you have

kid's molly?
　　　Chaos has a
home.

　　　Lord chaos
walks the earth,
next to allister-
six clawed, feline
in flea bitten
form. His mistress
temptress of the
night.

　　　T is 4 tool.
　　　Tonka trucks-
everyone must have
one.

　　　Die another
day.

　　　Taking care of
a baby Billy goat
for the aqua men
from Atlantis.

　　　They rose from
the deep to bring a
message of peace.

　　　Appearing to

me first in a
dream. The media
sensation has swept
the nation.

At first they
looked like tall
lanky black men in
strange white garb,
but upon further
inspection, by a
team of scientists,
their strange gills
became evident.
Build with the
ability to breath
in an out of water,
these strange me
have become all the
rage. A new
spectacle to behold
in a side circus.

The old man
hands one such man
an apple from the
felled tree. The
sugar twins watch
on.
"Johnny, "hit it in
the face!" Marie

smacks him in the
arm.

I hate myself.

I pull on my
underwear, the ones
with the Eiffel
tower on the
crotch.

F
i
n
.